THE MANY MOODS

OF THE

M
O
O
N

Shashank Mane

The Many Moods of the Moon

© Shashank Mane
Published by Rosetta Versos
Finland

© Rosetta Versos Kustantamo

We extend a special acknowledgment to Andy Willoughby
for his invaluable guidance in editing the poetry book
The Many Moods of the Moon.

Cover art / Kuvitus: Karita Forss
Graphic design / Graafinen suunnittelu: Rosetta Versos

Printed by: Libri Plureos GmbH, Hamburg, Germany

ISBN 978-952-65179-8-8 (kovakantinen)
ISBN 978-952-65179-9-5 (EPUB)
ISBN 978-952-7613-00-9 (PDF)

rosetta
VERSOS

Dedicated to my little Nona,
holder of my heart

Stand solid, my purple
my bruise, my rain

Stay strong, my orange
my torch, my flame

Remain intact, my black
my shade, my cover

Don't hurt, my blue
my deepest of lovers

My red, my fire
A silver I perspire

My green, my guts
eyes like apples I desire

Stand bold, my gold
autumn leaves over snow

Wrap around me like rainbows
and refuse to let me go

Today I swallowed a silver lining

My heart wore weakness to dinner
A suit freshly pressed of delicate fabrics
I had little to thicken the inner lining
a protruding rib sufficed to bulk me up
and push me out

I refrained from an appetizer
The moon's glow
borrowed for the main course
gleamed until I appeared
to have swallowed a million morsels
all to my heart's content

I was light
just as I ever was
filled with countless little particles
my head high in the clouds
with a stomach full of silver linings

My soul is scattered
across her shores and sands
inside her abandoned houses
and her warm valleys
on sun filled days

I wish to hold her close
when I catch her scent
in the air of the afternoon
light years away

I clutch onto her
a child refusing to leave his blanket
like rainwater upon mud
knowing we will dry up
eventually

I exist
cracked, firm
in spite of our separation

She is the passing of a life
A solitary salutation
in a cold place
the warmth in my infinite darkness

One day
I will walk across her endless highways
in the raindrops of her promised freedom
touching her colored skies
that I will once again
call home

For the human condition

What if I commit my crimes
in gentle tones
with hugs and warmth
where these sins have a home?

What if I summon my good deeds
during acts of corruption
counting all of my blessings
as I inflict destruction?

What if I suffocate the truth
as I praise its existence
the warmth of my skin beaming
against the clawing of truth's resistance?

What if I justify my conduct
with logic and sense
with science and facts
without need for pretense?

What if one day I finally awaken
in the silence of the meadows
to the warmth of the world's sunshine
to the wails of our broken widows?

What if I bury my demons
with a turn of the cheek?
what if my actions of deceit
were fully mine to keep?

Do you remember
when the orange ends of our cigarettes
charred the boundaries around our lives
burning holes into everything around us
ready to burst into a fireball
sparked simply by our inability to have any more
control
over its short fuse?

You always told me
to check the fingers on my hand
to lift them quickly over my eyes
and if I saw a finger too many
I was certain to be elsewhere
dreaming.

I don't remember why
you told me that life
at times could only be a lucid dream:
that our floating in outer space
amongst the stars and planets,
was a secret that many
simply didn't care to recognize.

I asked you once
what if we were just like birds
only our flight was more horizontal
more restricted than the others?
What if birds took a vertical route
in a different lane on the same highway?

I would tell you
of my world upside down
of my plans and their untimely deaths
before you would disappear
and I would float into the endless night-time
struggling to fall asleep.

The black curtain I had placed
over my bedroom windows
never kept me as safe
as the thought of seeing stars
speckled over the fabric of the darkened drapes
in the few seconds between being awake
and asleep.

I once had a dream
that I ran through thick snow blankets
of a strange distant wilderness,
never able to tell
if, in those brief seconds,
I was running towards or away
from everything I always wanted.

I no longer remember leaving
I only know
that if I had returned sooner
I might have remembered
that dreams die the slowest of deaths
only surviving upon the backs
of those desperate to live

Tonight,
I am still awake alone
in the bitter cold
surrounded by everything we always knew
everything that we always looked into
but when I raise my hands quickly over my eyes
I now see what was always there:
the silhouette of only five fingers
with nothing left to spare.

What
would need
to be seen all over again

if a lens could tell us
what it means to see
into the pores of our own skin?

A person angled
into a thousand dimensions
without a thought of definition

as an image played endlessly
would still be impossible
to find in a state of repetition

What if censored
if blurred
if distorted into the absurd

a picture could really speak
with the volume
of a thousand words?

Crimes captured
with the depth of artwork
imagined

life lived
in a series of moments
close captioned.

Attraction based
upon a million pixels
detailed

reruns of life
the validation
when all else has failed.

Spying
with the naked eye
everything never shown

an eye in the sky
unyielding
to a home never alone.

A room
without a window
is absence of blinding light

traded for the colors
of our brightest pictures
into a darkness out of sight.

The wings of fervor
upon these lips
carry sounds of excitement
into infinite darkness

The touches of flight
within these bones
take sensation to new heights
away into the galaxies

The feelings of fortitude
at our fingertips
mold steel into softness
caressing hardship into perspective

The sights of serenity
in our vision
turn desolation into beauty
every entity an artwork of excellence

The senses surrender
to the demands of our days
all the wonders in our vicinity
the objects of our fascination.

Purpose

When the winners go home
and we are left to our own devices
the nicest of our intentions
do little to console the depths of our sacrifices.

Grace is wrought from raw iron
every silent moment is a penance for trying
rising with our breaths, ambitions are still endless,
their pursuits without shame, infinite and lawless.

If a crawl to reach glory would suffice the soul
many would be happy to pursue their goals,
while much can be said of chasing a dream,
reality often has plans cutting down what they seem

I smash the pieces of my life to the ground without
worry,
knowing that I'll pick them up soon without
hurry,
If a lapse in intention is the judgment for some
we would all be at the mercy of being undone

There are many ways
to tell men apart:

their hair, their size,
words and eyes

their choice of curses,
taste in food -

if they relish silence
how they react to their mood,

how they spend their money
if they want to impress others,

if they're kind to their lovers,
how they treat their mothers,

are they vulgar?
are they sincere?

what few things
do they hold dear?

are they lazy?
are they stressed?

do they hoot and holler
at a woman in a tight dress?

some are generous,
some are austere,

some are hostile
when others come near

I don't know all
but I know a few

I might know enough about men
if I am to trust what they tell me to be true

men are nasty
men are nice

but they're just half the story
in the game of life.

Bring to me your light, your darkness, your soul in all
its fullness and scarcity
Let me touch this fabric of mind
Let me feel this sensation of thought
lay upon me your deepest of emptiness
your grayest of truths

So I may reveal to you your color of mind
So I can let you into our chequered coat
that shall cover us through the gates of sublimity
We may barter humility and exchange misunderstood
glances
For clarity shall prove all too simple, too easy, in our
confused world

Share vision, a common cause
"Lend me your ears", I once read
Shall we breathe, then, in unison, to infinite
capacities?
Let us be the great minds that think alike.

The Whip of Wisdom

I followed through a barrage of discomfort
from pain, from misery, from sadness
to a thousand lashes from the whip of wisdom
to make me a stronger and smarter being

I rise from the treachery of tyrannical lessons
to a simpler form of being, a sager eye through which
I see
I expect the hands of deceit to thrash me savage
but I am instead petted by the healing fingers of time

I endure hardships, I am graced with malice
exposed, disposed, imposed upon
but still I conquer, still I accomplish
even in defeat I am a victor standing fearless

I will overcome and continue to climb
only to be put down but I would still thrive
I will never give up, I shall not cease
Relentless in my pursuit of a life that I continue to
live and breathe.

The passing tragedy that is the life of others:
Is not ours as intact as the first kiss between lovers?

How it is, without a broken heart, to touch lips sealed
under moonlit covers
smothered, unconcerned under guises of one another?

What it is, to love fully

but those cruelly detached from Cupid's arrows
the marrow of human motive
bound to lessons in humility
living life single in sedentary silences bound to
frigidity

Love does not touch all, does not clutch on for long
Does not take us where we truly belong,
Does less right than it does wrong.

The unopened letters sealed under statements of
sentiment,
will they open into the arms of others or die away into
dust
met with earned distrust
to thrust away the ways of an affection so often unjust?

First and final act

Does my hope fade along the coasts of robust waves
of my youth-filled ways?
The gray that spurts with bitter wisdom
salting my pepper-colored hair
removing the flair from life, adding a touch of despair
to my mile long stare

I must contain, refrain from pleasure
like a human religious relic that discovers he is none
too clever.

Planted in the middle of a crowd
no longer standing proud, a notion of the past
like hands that removed the rains from the clouds
Hiding from the commotion that shall soon pass...
too fast, over my head, in an invisible shroud

Melancholy to counteract the folly of sense,
the madness in the hearts growing thick and dense
but I am brave despite our grave consequence
in silence, I remain, a wise adult to save my two cents

Defeated in purpose by these minutes of surplus
Curses in bold cursive birthing verses frantic and
nervous
These pages refuse to serve us, unnerve us in truths
and fervor
Left to murmurs of what was before time crushed all
upon its surface.

Rest assured peace shall not be found
Bound by the rotation of earth and repetition of a
world perhaps less profound
Down in our dumps, the thumps leave lasting lumps
on our days now numbered and numb
Dumbed down and smartened, disheartened and
sensible to a world so darkened like clouds.

Ticking clocks blunting shock stacked upon the
building blocks of man
Spanning wide and standing tall with a ball and chain
to refrain from pain staking plans
Deafened by mind, threatened in kind from behind
walls of the jilted and blind
Yet we find time within these moments to test what is
left in the best of our lasting lives.

Ordeals

The world may not compact your innumerable
experiences into a package deal.
Your soul may not be sold in order to reveal the true
nature of your ordeals.
The seal stamped by the state
A dream trampled
by men who hang on too long in a sickened, wrongful
debate
over our futures given away
instead of being led to create.

Dare to build on your humbling, decide to progress
instead of stumbling down the wrong path.
We, the artists, must stay as sharp as our tools, as
brushes, instruments and pens that gruel into the
dusty pool
of life's bloody duels against us in wrath.

I jump into the light at the end of the tunnel
finally funnelled into the channels
of existence in this lonely jungle.
The essence of our suffering ushers light
onto the works of dark days
transforming our meager work into sharp displays
of art in magnificent ways.

It is not the ordeals that make us so for there is no key
that opens the world of our tinted glow.
So we embark on this journey
that carries upon our vessels of choice
through the world's turbulent flow.
And continue to grow
despite everything that life may have to throw
gathering in spite to delight and rejoice.

The morning light carving shapes of shadows onto
my bedroom walls
the patterns without sense, I find a darkness to lie
within
in my world of wake ups, the morning make-up of
dew and the sunshine springs me to the warmth of life

But when I awaken to the covering of clouds and dark
matters that project from the skies
I wish for warmth, for the splashes of sun to cover the
breadth of my neighborhood and beyond
My coffee filters. It is never long.
The weather was forecast as such. The sun stretches
and I forget to complain about the rest.

What do I await? A plate prepared from the hands of
altered fate?
I will reach out into the day to walk between the
droplets of rain staining my jacket. The skies are
covered in shining mist as before. The day is to be
taken and the weather, forsaken.

Captivity

Outrage
in cages where we sit
faces charred
in dark corners
ordered for confinement
but free as birds we shall be
when the windows to the soul
reveal the untold
to those who peer
into the cells of our imagination
for a tragic creation in captivity.

The quiet
sly lens
of silence
captures soliloquy stylists
smiling less
in fits of shyness

But it will be a while
before a warm touch and smile
tears open mouths
and the cold cracks around raw lip corners
offer a warm touch and smile.

Reflections

You may not know
but you may look my way
for the reflection in the glass
may distort what you see
and forever my display

For whatever reason you wish not to look
for fear, for shame
for you might be mistook
I'll take a chance and keep looking in your direction
and you might consider me crass
or mistake my eyes for an inspection

...but how those eyes...stay averted and shy
how those cheeks turn with pride, away to the side
you may be correct that I needed a second glance
did you know that strangers meet by chance?
but only if first they wish to dance.

I watch the winds howl through the trees
I see my needs flung high
stung, sung by triumphant breeze.
My wants they come by
sometimes
but my sunshine
she comes and goes
through the creeks and groves
for a lifetime, as she may please.

Dark Leaves

Smoking sensational paragraphs to burn away at the
filter between mouth and mind
indulging in exotic flavors, rolled between papers for
these rhymes written and left behind,
passing through hands before bidding goodbye
through clouds of smoke.
The pounds of paragraphs trickle away into scenes of
perpetual night seeping out of imperfect throats.

Into the sway of palm trees cold against the dark seas
where the cold moonlight meets the heart on my
warm sleeves,
a place for thieves to eavesdrop, only to catch wind
of the passing of minds between these smoked leaves
to stay somber a little longer, for our words are
stronger than what our minds perceive.

Dry cotton begotten on the tips of tongues and inner
cheeks,
filling the lungs with silence, strung on clouds high
as ice tipped peaks
exhaling the trailing sounds of the ailing, to send
sailing our thoughts lost for weeks
between the dark nights through which I sleep, and
the brighter days forever mine to keep.

Give up
Quit
Lay down
Split

Into little pieces
saddened and cracked
broken without repair
uncomfortable and flat on your back

Try to rise but you cannot move
Try to dance but you will not groove
Fall into step, join the crowd
Call in sick
But hold onto all that is proud

Accomplishments and achievements
the refreshing of bereavements
pain and hardship
in the face of life's disagreements

Inconvenient methods
for flawed results
should you succumb now
or wait for more insults

Adults overwhelmed
roughed up for good measure
but there within lies our pearl
for the high standards of worldly treasure.

Liberation

In hopes of escape
I leap over mountains
I jump across bridges
And run through the plains

In hopes of escape
I leave behind the loved
I lock all doors and swallow keys
I run for the hills
Far away from the life I perceive

In hopes of freedom
I chase the stars in the sky
I fly as far as the eye
Never to understand or truly know why

In hopes of freedom
I gallop like horses
I leap and bolt like foxes
to run free for all that life offers

My feet will carry me
As far as I can go
As far as the world can throw me
As long as I no longer show

But I will never be free
As I will never live in peace
Never to find a peace of mind
Never to forget everything I leave behind.

Roads
take their leave with time.
The evening traffic lights stagger between red and
green
And the few pedestrians try to walk safe
through the night.
When do I get to travel
this road I created for myself?
When the potholes and red lights are the only
memory
and the rain and cold streets
are the lonely scenery?

When do I slam on the brakes
to stop and enjoy the best of the views?
When do I take my chosen path
and ride to where I please and choose?

I cruise behind the wheel
to steal a pleasant sight
The sleepy curve of my eyelids
do little to shield me from the oncoming lights

I can be wrong and go astray
driving to where I think I belong
The streets are often old
and the paths are never long.

Lucky as I ever was
to get on these highways of life
It was a simple trip I chose
Going to the places I contrived with my eyes.

When daybreak hits
I am one of many on this open road
but at night, I'm alright and alone
when I travel free in the lightness in which I roam.

How birds learn to fly

One day I saw a bird
I watched her flap her wings and walk on her little
legs
she pecked and foraged, she pointed her beak at
scraps of food.
The cars drove by but she didn't flinch much or move
eating what she could find
finding out quickly what she could and couldn't do.

She soon found a mate
and then had babies
Waddling along so gently
their flock of plenty

I counted nine but there were more
they walked in line
and lived and swam together by the shore

When I went down to the bay
I watched them float
one by one, the row of ducks
hovering over water, swayed by the currents
the boats raced past
and they clung close by the dozen

When I saw them last
they looked happy as could be
quacking and flapping, the two ducks and their babies

But when I counted the ducklings, I could not see
I saw one, I saw two, and finally, I only saw three.

How nice and fine it would be
to be a bird of the sea
How nice and easy it must be
to flutter my wings and think I was free

They tear through us
ripping dignity from our minds
a word at a time.

Covered in the imprints of destitution
we are committed to conform
each breath a mirror of their ways.

Outdated, outstretched
laid to rest in perfect peace
if we were never to close our eyes
our problems would never cease.

The world knows us as outsiders
we've been here all along
for years in the same position
still we wonder where we belong,

if everything is wrong -
The good in us has gone sour,
the world was once a nice place
never once when it was all ours.

Just being

The price of life
is worth a pittance,
existence on earth
is the offered remittance.

Inside the belly of the betrayed
forever an emptiness unfulfilled
within the depths of our humanity
a shrill sanity we never hesitate to spill.

Stand tall upon the water's edge
never to dry inside
dig through the wells of weight within
gather the ounces of pride,

Settle upon the solids -
life can be a complicated affair.
Strong are the souls who hold firm
without need to ever despair

Satisfied is the being
submitting to the scope of perspective.
Lucky is the man who discovers
he is compensated by every wrong corrected.

There are millions of smiling faces on earth
I can no longer seem to see -
a million happier people by birth
I no longer need to try and be.

I am as simple as a passing breeze
with a heart that bends through words like rivers
Gushing over to the fringes
how I pass through the desperation overcome
never without a thoughtful mind overrun

If I was complicated
I would suffer further with time
Falling deeper into my mind
Choked over the years
by debating the power
of distinction undefined

Around my throat
are signs of vivid breath
The air seeping slowly
in and out of my heaving chest

At best I am calm
At worst, my own enemy
Simple men are easy to please
Knowing they will pass on eventually

Upon the canvas of my eye

Dreaming upon the stars
through the days and nights
in the afternoons and evenings
in between the visions
preoccupying my sights

I sit and wonder
daydream and ponder
render actions into endless thought
oh, this wonderful freedom of mind
I don't think it can ever be bought

Head down or held high
into the ground or up in the sky
through galaxies and universes
and the black holes swallowing whole
the figments filtering in through my eyes

I awake in strange places unknown
Every morning under the warm sheets on my bed
I wonder where I am when I'm alone
not always within grasp or touch
but always somewhere inside the confines of my head

The colors are fuller here
The scenery to my taste
Take it slow and let it go
Didn't you already know?
A mind is a beautiful thing to waste

Sea shells upon the sands hold sounds of the ocean
People in turmoil embrace stories of the broken
Waves crashing and smashing upon the coast
Threaten to take away what we endear the most
The stories from our breaths left unaccounted like
ghosts

Endless fights and scars ill-repaired
The lower you stoop, the more you find that people
grin and bear
Life is unfair and there is little we try to do
Let the walls break down to the ground
to create something beautiful between me and you

We can burrow and dig until little is left to uncover
Harrowing details of tales of one another
The things we do to each other in the name of
vengeance
They say revenge is best served cold
but it is warmth that preserves the essence of our
friendships

Where I left of

Isn't it something to wish
that tomorrow could be chosen as a dish today
and I could go on fishing away the remaining minutes
giving up if I dare?
To face today knowing tomorrow
would have nothing to spare.

Isn't it something to want?
our pasts gaunt and disintegrated,
thinking away the memories wished upon
and slated to thieve me
would no longer grieve
and simply get up and one day leave me

The problem has always been
that, although it is long over,
we are still standing
inside each other
looking, watching, listening
breathing our presence
in crowded spaces and tiny rooms
in neither of which
elephants have ever fit
but still sit
awaiting a train
that refuses to move along.

Freedom

I am a feather
detached from body and wing
grounded and alive
to what this world may bring.

When I am flung from place to place
landing where the wind may take me
without baggage to lift
I'm free to be whatever it may make me.

Isn't there something about the night time breeze
carrying you to me
through a corridor of rooms
in the confines of weightless darkness?

The blinds shake with your passing steps
and my heart jumps
with every stuttering memory I've kept
locked inside the walls of these rooms.

The curtains quiver
like a bird with its wings clipped,
Fluttering in the twilight
holding on to the withered walls against which they
hang.

It isn't long
before you fade into the winds
and I am left alone to wonder
when I will hear your steps again.

To let them be

Is it love they so woefully crave?
or are the seeds sprinkled over the pauper's grave
blooming into life ripped from a sorrowful page?

Stricken into poverty, the mud of life
clings tight within fists
until clumps of cold stone and earth are hurled
doing little to move the ground beneath their feet
as it shifts.

Yet the gloom covered within the fog, the bogged
down,
the hopped and bartered logs of life are always
mangled,
tangled within a web of knives.
Must they be picked and cut
to unveil the eyes of a forest full of silent cries?

There are things that are lost
that can never again be found
as there are things I have found,
that are better off forgotten and drowned

Crowded alone upon the throne of the lost,
forgotten at all costs -
the price of brooding and braving,
engraving life upon the seas of all that is soft.

I lift my cup
and tilt the oceans
to push memories out
and remembrances of devotion.

What spills out into our world
is not the concern of the stars,
What stays planted below the surface
is never out of reach or far.

Hangman

Only when I have eaten enough
will I sit down quietly
to eat my own words

I will gnaw and savor
and chew on each sentence
until I swallow the alphabet strewn
across my palette
and satisfy my stomach
with the kicks delivered
by each beautiful letter.

I know how this ends
with little money
and fewer friends.

You know how this ends
how you always wanted it to
without the pomp and frills
and the thrills of pretend.

They know how this ends
always by your side, family and company forever
The terror in their eyes watching you disappear
into a slow break and bend.

We know how this ends
yet we move forward
onward, up and out of sight into the grips
of forever without repair.

Wishlist

I walk without and talk about
a face I wish I had
with teeth and nose and lips and mouth
so I chalk around my head and hands
and stalk around my friends who have
a face so graceful, a face so tasteful
a head, a neck, a body and plan
but I have no face so all be damned
I will search and command and conquer
and stand
as a man with a face

but oh how I would wear such a face so grand!

I have created a mass outside myself
It breathes and it lives. It sees and it can smell

It lives where I dwell, to my six, it is twelve
to something small, it is large and for a high road it is
hell.

This mass is a black hole, a whirlpool of currents
pushing and pulling, the mass is master and I am
servant

It watches me move and it gives me space
to this mass I must prove that I exist without face

I have done little wrong but guilty I am
This mass is the judgment of the filthy and damned

The mass will watch and the mass will record
When I am full of energy, the mass will absorb

Absolved and free but with this darkness by my side
my black hole, my black mass,
ready and willing to feed on my pride

"It is not real, it is not real" I slither
spineless like an eel
my dark mass must know everything I know and how
I feel
The mass will kick me down and the mass will watch
me lay
a drop of blood amongst the billions for the mass won't
let me stay

Class

I dismantle my education
to build mistrust

sweep with my fingers the dust
under clean carpets of the just

I uncover truth aplenty
only to stir emptiness
as thick as gales and gusts.

A cold calculation
like the souls of old men
swilling sips of malice

Words flow freely from embittered mouths
for it is only truth
that may spill into the eternal balance.

I did not know that it could fly
that it could soar, how it could cry

I never saw it fall but I saw it try
to stand back up and take to the sky

I watched it hobble over mud and grass
Some of us live long and some of us live fast

I watched it wobble from inside my walls
It tried to stand tall

It turned around when I could no longer look
It didn't stand a chance, it didn't have what it took

Life is short and for some it is shorter
Some are walked to their slaughter but this one
simply walked away into dark waters.

We wish to see the young grow, we walk amiss
among friend and foe
The bird waddled away like a little baby with webbed
feet like little toes

I never saw it again and never happened to really
know
It was only an infant, a baby bird perhaps, yet
destined for a little growth.

Lucid

There are days when the sky displays
a lack of ways to find my stars,
So I sift through the clouds
when they start to come around,
pushing my hand through to find where they are.

There are times when I fall behind
slumbering in sleep so deep,
but I shake myself awake
and realize the bed is a mistake,
when I talk in sleep so sound
about answers that cannot be found.

There are minutes I sit and wonder
about life in all its thunder and rain,
but I am quick to change my mind
in fear of being left behind -
so I try to run away
but get stuck in place all the same.

My shopping list stays the same over time
The only thing expanding besides my debt
is the circumference of my waistline.

My income it seldom grows
but losses tend to be incurred
and the line between states of plenty and meager
remain forever blurred,

I met the rich and many acted poor
and when I met the poor, they never let on
when they couldn't really afford any more.

The trouble ahead
I can always predict
but the minutes and seconds that I live in
never seem to move fast and forward as the clock
ticks.....

I wait for time to run its course but I run in place with
fire and force,
the shackles are broken and change will come
but I've seen it before
wedged between weary and numb.

Pushed and shoved

You were the inclement weather
the tangled tether, the bad to the better
the odd number to beautiful letters

A bully so bold
in a world so cold
How you folded under their pressure
traded all your treasures
for a bite into warm souls
pushing and shoving us for personal pleasure

The frail steel cot I slept on as a child
The plastic toys I flung and the wooden bats I swung
over and over to make some kind of dent within the
world in the wild

The countless glasses that slipped from my fingers to
the floor
the endless pairs of headphone wires
that could no longer play sweet voices within my ears
anymore

The bottles of beer we drank and smashed to the
ground together
the sweat from our foreheads
Laughing until we broke out into tears forever

The clouds when I wished it would never stop raining
My concentration when the thoughts within my mind
wished themselves forever into a state of waning

The countless pencil tips
that I broke every time I tried to write
The rules of magic
even when they failed to trick our little sight
My gaze when I looked up at the stars
The skin which I'm reminded of
when I look down on my scars

The waves from the moon and the laws of nature
but I never played a part in shaping those
The tattered rose when I clipped its stem
The ice when everything between us
should have remained frozen within

Crows

A network is bred through necessity
to provide opportunity
and resources
to form a community.

We are dark and conspicuous
like sore thumbs against a backdrop
of fresh blades of green grass
and perfect, tidy shrubs.

Crows are known to alert one another
when they sense imminent danger
or passing threat.

Crows remember faces
their memory serving as a radar
recording past infringements
imposed by humans
and other animals.

When I'm alone in the evening
merging gently into the cold night
when my family is out of reach
and my friends have gone to sleep,
I always hope
to stumble upon a murder of crows
to remind me
that no matter the distance
between me and the world,
there are still eyes
watching me move
lingering quietly beside me
in the weight of my darkness.

My crystal ball never tells me
of all it needs to show
how I fall, how I grow
how I could see it all coming
how little I really know.

My crystal ball asks me questions
the answers are always formality
in actuality, the ball laughs cynically
points ahead to the future
following behind me in mimicry.

I always consider
if my eyes can endure the ball without blinking
If I can continue and go on free thinking.
Whether I can live as if I have always lived
without true knowledge or even an inkling?

My ball clouds up, my ball clears
my ball traces around everything that I hold dear
the ball never falls because the ball can never be
dropped
the ball keeps me rolling over
the ball can never be stopped

I can never run from the ball
we are polar opposites like spring and fall
the ball ends curiosity giving life to schemes
the ball promises hope
the ball might choose silence if it can't hear me
scream.

I rub the crystal ball at times
hoping for knowledge of our relations
the ball always reminds me of patience
begs silence to any elation
the chain holding us together in damnation

If I was ever to write you

I would write you a sweet song
as long as you let me tag along
to hum your tune to the world

I would write you a sweet song
to sing you my wrongs
to free you into flight like birds

If I write a song
to tell you all
I would remove the weight of all words

When I finally write
I'll tell you what it's like
sharing in your dreams which I serve

I would write you a melody
whistle into your ears a soft remedy
to free you from troubles and pains

I would jot down our notes
repeat their harmony through my throat
to hold us together in one and the same

As long as you're light
a true source of my life
I would cherish your breath and your beat

Off your feet, I would uplift you
carrying you into a world they would gift you
To make you forget the gravity at your feet.

They tell me this is earth
a name given formally
we are all called by something
as the humans we were born to be

We are given arms and legs
to be standard and not an anomaly
We are given a nationality
with hopes of peace and normalcy

We are expected to follow a script
To grasp knowledge and know laws,
we're told to sit in a room with others
to have answers and not to talk

We are reminded that it is all real
that consequences in life are grave
that now people are all free and paid
that we aren't slaves but part of free trade

We are covered in a mask of skin
with faces and a range of features,
we are asked to be something
to contribute as doctors and teachers

When we were children and asked
"What are we doing here?"
We were told to keep quiet
"...and please sit still, my dear"

Now we act like we don't know
That there is nothing we have really seen
That it is what it is
instead of the million things it could have been.

Her beautiful hair

My girl
do you know
that Samson's source of strength
was not his glow?
It wasn't his sword
it wasn't his bow
how hard he could throw
where his chariots would let him go.

If your hair was ever meant to be stolen
it would repel all thieves
because you gather the enchanted looks of lovers
the warmth of mothers
and the longing gaze of all the others

Your eyes match
like those little socks upon your skin
your hair at your command and whim
dropping over your eyes forming a little fringe

When I rub my hand over your head
I think the least of any betrayal
one day you might be a grandmother
still never will your hair be old and frail.

If I had a million black strands of hair
not one would be as wonderful as yours
If your hair was something that Samson ever saw

it would have sufficed to stop all of Samson's wars.

When I was a child
I would awake
thrust into the midst of the nighttime ocean

A gasp of air
when I broke through the water's surface
my only lasting memory

I always wished I had seen
a buoy or a beacon of light
somewhere in the distance
for comfort and reassurance
in the surrounding vastness.

The salt water waves
colliding against my skin
The tar oil glimmer of the ocean
beating against my struggling body

my eyes briefly opening
into the endless moment.

Now, when I awake stranded between continents
floating upon the surface of water
without sight of land
I look up at the stars
when I emerge from the bottomless ocean

knowing that I will find your pupils
in those few precious seconds
amongst the million fiery little dots of light

glittering
        like
                black pearls
                        in the midnight sky

CONTENTS

For my many moods   7
Today I swallowed a silver lining   8
Home   9
For the human condition   10
If you were one day willing to see   11-12
A room without a view   13-14
Senses   15
Purpose   16
The ways of man   17-18
To get her   19
The Whip of Wisdom   20
To live in love   21
First and final act   22
A lesson in time   23
Ordeals   24
Autumn alarm clock   25
Captivity   26
All Smiles   27
Reflections   28
Going   29
Dark Leaves   30
Failure   31
Liberation   32
Evening Lights   33
How birds learn to fly   34
With and without us   35
Just being   36
Simple breaths   37
Upon the canvas of my eye   38
Swallowed stories   39
Where I left of   40

The Last Station   41

Freedom   42

Footsteps in the wind 43

To let them be   44

Empty pockets   45

Hangman   46

For the destined   47

Wishlist   48

Mass   49

Class   50

Broken Birds   51

Lucid   52

Unpaid debts   53

Pushed and shoved   54

Things I didn't mean to break   55

Crows   56

A Telling Tale   57

If I was ever to write you   58

Standard deviations   59

Her beautiful hair   60

The open skies   61

rosetta
VERSOS

Milton Keynes UK
Ingram Content Group UK Ltd.
UKHW050055271124
451586UK00008B/81

9 789526 517988